anythink

D0604383

OUR
GREAT
STATES

WHAT'S GREAT ABOUT

ILLINOIS?

✴ Kristin Marciniak

LERNER PUBLICATIONS ✴ MINNEAPOLIS

CONTENTS

ILLINOIS
WELCOMES YOU! ✳ 4

Content Consultant: W. Michael Weis, PhD,
Professor of History, Illinois Wesleyan
University

Lerner Publications Company
A division of Lerner Publishing Group, Inc.
241 First Avenue North
Minneapolis, MN 55401 USA

For reading levels and more information, look
up this title at www.lernerbooks.com.

Main body text set in ITC Franklin Gothic Std
Book Condensed 12/15.
Typeface provided by Adobe Systems.

Library of Congress Cataloging-in-Publication
Data

Marciniak, Kristin.
    What's great about Illinois? / by Kristin
Marciniak.
        pages   cm. — (Our great states)
    Includes index.
    ISBN 978-1-4677-3867-5 (lib. bdg. :
alk. paper)
    ISBN 978-1-4677-6269-4 (eBook)
    1. Illinois—Juvenile literature. I. Title.
F541.3.M37 2015
977.3—dc23   2014017302

Manufactured in the United States of America
1 – PC – 12/31/14

ILLINOIS Welcomes You!

Illinois is the Land of Lincoln. President Abraham Lincoln lived here before moving into the White House. Illinois is also known for its major city: Chicago. Chicago has many fun places to visit, including the world's largest indoor aquarium. But there's much to see and do outside of the city. Some call Illinois the Prairie State. Illinois has beautiful prairies and cliffs, as well as ancient mounds to investigate. It's the home of a famous highway and a superhero who wears an *S* on his chest. So what are you waiting for? Let's explore Illinois!

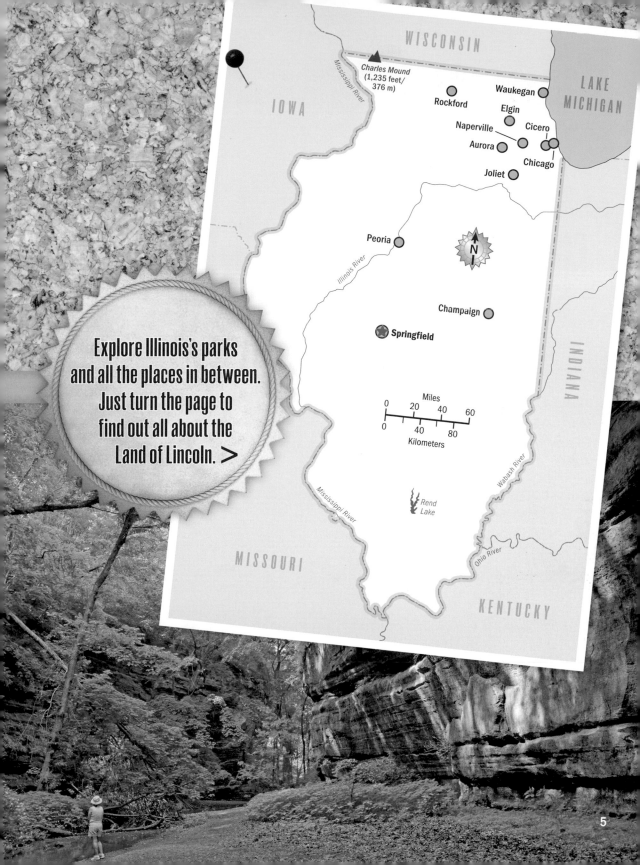

WISCONSIN

LAKE
MICHIGAN

IOWA

Mississippi River

Charles Mound
(1,235 feet/
376 m)

Rockford

Waukegan

Elgin

Naperville

Cicero

Aurora

Chicago

Joliet

Peoria

Illinois River

N

Champaign

Springfield

INDIANA

Miles
0   20   40   60
0   40   80
Kilometers

Mississippi River

Rend
Lake

Wabash River

MISSOURI

Ohio River

KENTUCKY

Explore Illinois's parks
and all the places in between.
Just turn the page to
find out all about the
Land of Lincoln. >

CHICAGO'S MUSEUMS

> Start your Illinois adventure at the Shedd Aquarium in Chicago. Here, you'll see more than eight thousand aquatic animals. View sharks and coral reefs. Touch sea stars at the Polar Play Zone. Climb inside a small submarine to see beluga whales. Or try on a penguin suit and pretend to be a penguin!

Next, head over to the Field Museum. Be sure to say hello to Sue. She's the largest *Tyrannosaurus rex* skeleton in the world. Then peek in on some Egyptian mummies. Or head into Underground Adventure. See the world as a bug would see it as you walk through soil tunnels. There is even a giant penny to touch.

Set aside plenty of time for the Museum of Science and Industry. Stand next to a 40-foot-tall (12-meter) tornado. Find your favorite fairy-tale character in the enormous Fairy Castle dollhouse. Don't forget to visit the baby chicks in the hatchery!

CASIMIR PULASKI DAY

Chicago has a very strong Polish heritage. The city celebrates Casimir Pulaski Day on the first Monday in March. Pulaski was a Polish immigrant. He heard about the Revolutionary War (1775–1783) and wanted to help the Americans fight. He became a great leader but died after being wounded in battle. This holiday honors what Pulaski did for his new country.

Sue, the largest *Tyrannosaurus rex* skeleton in the world, is 42 feet (13 m) long and 12 feet (4 m) tall.

JOHN G. SHEDD AQUARIUM

CELEBRATE 75 SHEDD AQUARIUM

WRIGLEY FIELD

> Are you a Chicago Cubs fan? If so, chances are you won't root for the Chicago White Sox. Few sports rivalries are as old as theirs. Catch a Cubs game at the historic Wrigley Field. Or take a tour and sit in the dugout. Did you know Wrigley Field was the first ballpark to let fans keep foul balls? Maybe you'll even be able to catch a souvenir!

Chicago is a sports lover's dream come true. Are you a basketball fan? Then a Chicago Bulls basketball game at the United Center is the place to be. Do you like hockey? The Chicago Blackhawks also play here. And if you love soccer, make sure to catch a Chicago Fire game at Toyota Park.

Wrigley Field was built in 1914, making it the second-oldest ballpark in the United States.

Football fans can head to Soldier Field to watch the Chicago Bears play football.

STARVED ROCK STATE PARK

> In 2012, Starved Rock State Park was voted the best place to see in Illinois. This park in Utica is home to eighteen canyons and fourteen waterfalls. It also has 13 miles (21 kilometers) of hiking trails. Follow the path and the wooden stairs to the top of Starved Rock. At 125 feet (38 m) aboveground, it is the park's biggest bluff. You'll have a good view of the nearby hills and fields. Head back down to fish and boat on the Illinois River.

The park is home to many kinds of wildlife. If you visit in the winter, keep your eyes peeled for bald eagles. The park hosts a special weekend to celebrate these birds each January. In the warmer months, search for moles, deer, wood ducks, and beavers.

Go on a tour to scout for bald eagles at Starved Rock State Park.

SANDSTONE CANYONS

The canyons at Starved Rock State Park are made of sandstone. Sandstone is a kind of rock made of sand-like grains. The sandstone is all that is left of a huge inland sea that was here 425 million years ago. Glaciers eventually covered the sandstone. When the glaciers melted, the sandstone was left on the surface. Streams feed into the Illinois River and cut through the sandstone. These streams have eroded the rock to create the canyons.

JOHN DEERE PAVILION

> Can you remember the color of the last tractor you saw? If it was green, it was a John Deere tractor. John Deere's bright green tractors and combines are in fields around the world. Moline is the home of John Deere. Get up close and personal with these green machines at the John Deere Pavilion. Make sure someone snaps a picture as you crawl inside the tree feller's massive wheels. They are each 5.4 feet (1.6 m) tall!

One of the biggest pieces of equipment here is the combine. Climb the stairs into the cab. Get comfy in the driver's seat. Count the many buttons and levers in the cab. Can you imagine what it's like to drive this beast through a cornfield? Practice harvesting crops on one of the simulators. Who knew farming could be this much fun?

Climb in and test the controls on your favorite John Deere tractors.

JOHN DEERE

Illinois was a great place for settlers to start farms in the 1800s. The rich soil was perfect for growing crops. The settlers used cast iron tools. These tools had worked well in the light, sandy soil in the East. But they didn't work so well in the heavy prairie soil of Illinois. In 1837, blacksmith John Deere found a solution. He built a plow made of polished steel. The thick Illinois soil slid right off. Farming on the prairie was suddenly much easier. Deere sold his plows and other tools to farmers. His creations changed farming forever.

WILDLIFE PRAIRIE STATE PARK

Look for black bear cubs on your train ride through Wildlife Prairie State Park.

> Before Illinois was settled, the territory was covered with open prairie. Much of the prairie has been turned into cities and towns. But some of it remains in Hanna City at Wildlife Prairie State Park. Wildlife Prairie State Park covers 2,000 acres (809 hectares). Take a ride on the Prairie Zephyr Train. Spot some of the 150 animals living here. You might see bison, elk, wolves, and even cougars.

After your train ride, explore the walking and biking trails. Be sure to take a turn on the 60-foot-long (18 m) slide built into a hillside. After the sun sets, spend the night at the park. Choose from a cottage, cabin, train caboose, or horse barn. Don't worry. They all have beds—even the barn.

HOME ON THE PRAIRIE

Illinois became a territory in 1809. It was named a state in 1818. The earliest settlers made their homes in the south. At the time, southern Illinois was covered with trees. Settlers had to cut down trees to make room for fields and farming. Why didn't they settle on the open prairies in other parts of the state? The settlers thought nothing would grow there. They were wrong. By the mid-1800s, central Illinois was known for its farmland. Immigrants from all around the world came to live and farm here.

MORTON PUMPKIN FESTIVAL

> Welcome to Morton, Illinois, the Pumpkin Capital of the World! Here, the Libby's pumpkin plant produces more than 80 percent of the world's canned pumpkin. That's a lot of pumpkin! Canned pumpkin is used to make all kinds of yummy goodies, including pumpkin pie. The pumpkin pie you enjoyed at Thanksgiving could have come from Morton.

Visit in fall for the Morton Pumpkin Festival. You can enter the "hand-tossed" category of the Punkin Chuckin' contest. See how far you can throw a pumpkin. After you smash a few pumpkins, sit back and watch kids and adults show off their punkin chuckin' machines. Some pumpkins fly as far as 2,000 feet (610 m)! Plan ahead and build a catapult with some friends. Can you chuck your pumpkin the farthest?

Pick out your own pumpkin for chuckin' or carving at the Morton Pumpkin Festival.

Watch catapults and air cannons shoot pumpkins through the air.

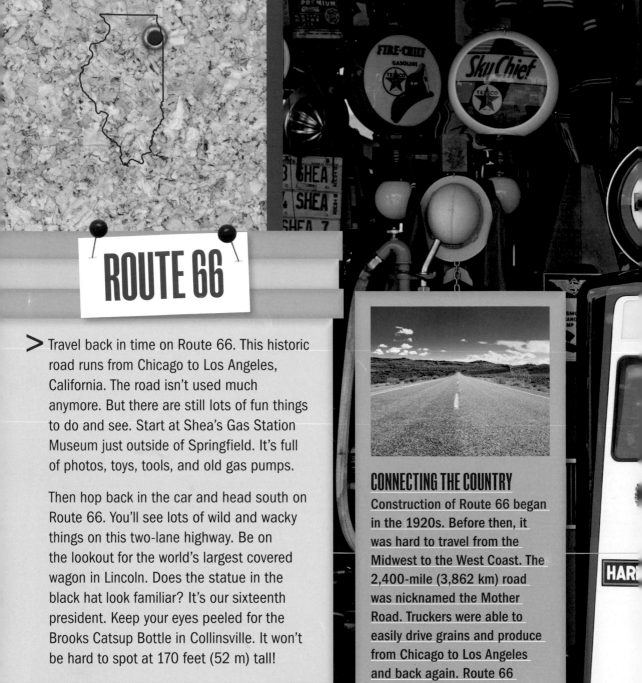

ROUTE 66

> Travel back in time on Route 66. This historic road runs from Chicago to Los Angeles, California. The road isn't used much anymore. But there are still lots of fun things to do and see. Start at Shea's Gas Station Museum just outside of Springfield. It's full of photos, toys, tools, and old gas pumps.

Then hop back in the car and head south on Route 66. You'll see lots of wild and wacky things on this two-lane highway. Be on the lookout for the world's largest covered wagon in Lincoln. Does the statue in the black hat look familiar? It's our sixteenth president. Keep your eyes peeled for the Brooks Catsup Bottle in Collinsville. It won't be hard to spot at 170 feet (52 m) tall!

CONNECTING THE COUNTRY

Construction of Route 66 began in the 1920s. Before then, it was hard to travel from the Midwest to the West Coast. The 2,400-mile (3,862 km) road was nicknamed the Mother Road. Truckers were able to easily drive grains and produce from Chicago to Los Angeles and back again. Route 66 also opened the door for the American road trip. Exploring the United States was as simple as hopping into the family station wagon.

The Railsplitter Covered Wagon in Lincoln measures 40 feet (12 m) long, 24 feet (7 m) tall, and 12 feet (4 m) wide.

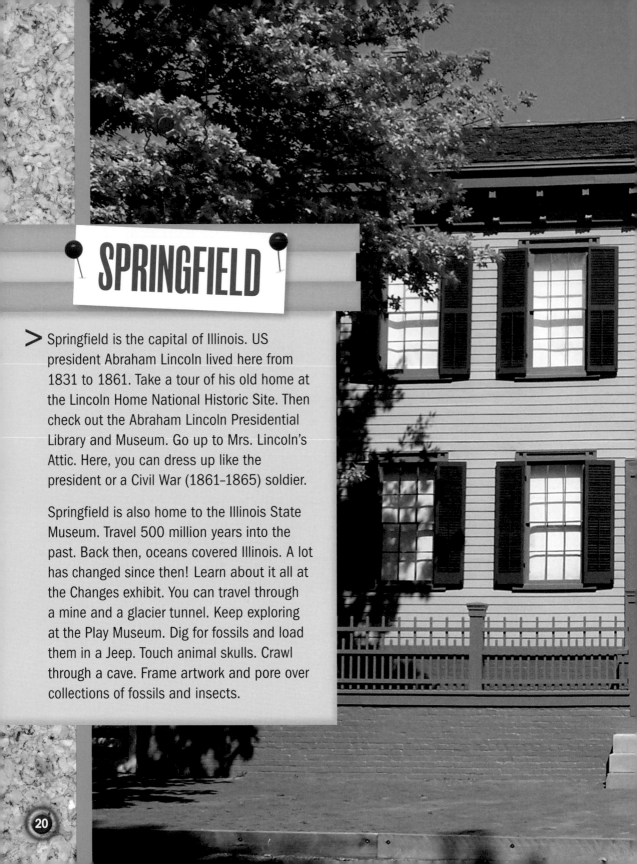

SPRINGFIELD

> Springfield is the capital of Illinois. US president Abraham Lincoln lived here from 1831 to 1861. Take a tour of his old home at the Lincoln Home National Historic Site. Then check out the Abraham Lincoln Presidential Library and Museum. Go up to Mrs. Lincoln's Attic. Here, you can dress up like the president or a Civil War (1861–1865) soldier.

Springfield is also home to the Illinois State Museum. Travel 500 million years into the past. Back then, oceans covered Illinois. A lot has changed since then! Learn about it all at the Changes exhibit. You can travel through a mine and a glacier tunnel. Keep exploring at the Play Museum. Dig for fossils and load them in a Jeep. Touch animal skulls. Crawl through a cave. Frame artwork and pore over collections of fossils and insects.

Take a picture with statues of Lincoln and his family at the Abraham Lincoln Presidential Library and Museum.

See what it's like to work at a museum at the Play Museum exhibit at the Illinois State Museum.

CAHOKIA MOUNDS

> The next stop is Collinsville. More than twelve hundred years ago, this southern city was called Cahokia. An unknown American Indian tribe built this city of mounds in 700 CE. More than twenty thousand people lived here in 1250. By 1400, the city was deserted. Only the tall, grassy plateaus remain.

Begin your visit at the Cahokia Mounds State Historic Site and Interpretive Center. Study models of the ancient city to learn how the mounds were built. Then head outside and explore the mounds. Be on the lookout for Woodhenge. It's an outdoor calendar made of wooden poles.

End your visit by climbing all 154 steps to the top of Monks Mound. It is 100 feet (30 m) tall and covers 14 acres (6 hectares). That makes it the largest prehistoric earthwork in the Americas.

THE MISSING MOUNDS

There were once 120 mounds in Cahokia. Only 69 remain. The missing mounds were flattened in the early 1900s. Most of them were taken down and replaced with houses, businesses, and an airfield. Many of the mounds that are left are protected as part of a state historic site. You can't climb on the grassy hillsides. Too much foot traffic would erode the mounds. That's why each one has stairs.

Shadows from Woodhenge's poles may have once helped tell people what day it was.

METROPOLIS

> Don't forget to visit Metropolis before leaving Illinois. The most famous resident of Metropolis actually began his life on another planet. He usually goes by the name Clark Kent. You might know him better as Superman. When the *Superman* comic books were first published in 1938, Clark Kent lived in a made-up city called Metropolis. In 1972, the people of Metropolis, Illinois, adopted the Man of Steel as their own.

Superman's face is all over town. Stop at the Super Museum. It has more than one hundred thousand pieces of Superman memorabilia. Browse through action figures, lunch boxes, and costumes. Be sure to visit Clark's hometown during the Superman Celebration in June. This event is held every year. It's a lot like a county fair. It has carnival rides, a fun run, and Superman-themed games.

YOUR TOP TEN

Now that you've read about ten awesome things to see and do in Illinois, think about what your Illinois top ten list would include. What would you be most excited about if you were planning an Illinois vacation? What do you want to see? These are questions to consider as you think about your own top ten. Make your list on a separate sheet of paper. You can even turn your list into a book. You can add drawings or pictures from the Internet or magazines.

Get your picture taken with the 15-foot-tall (5 m) Superman statue that watches over the town square.

Hop into the official Superman phone booth and pretend you're changing into a superhero costume of your own.

ILLINOIS BY MAP

> MAP KEY

⭐ Capital city

⭕ City

◯ Point of interest

🔺 Highest elevation

—·— State border

—— Route 66

ILLINOIS

Visit www.lerneresource.com to learn
more about the state flag of Illinois.

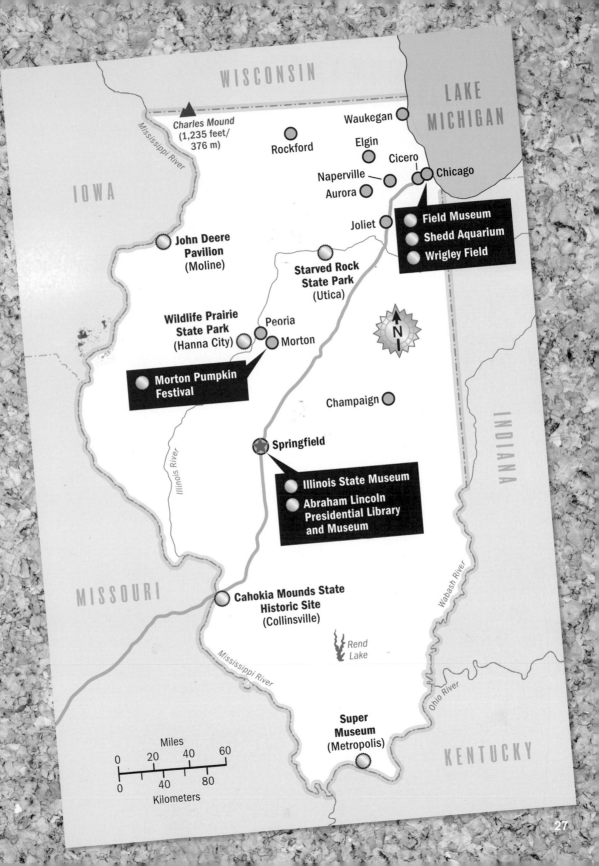

WISCONSIN

LAKE MICHIGAN

IOWA

Mississippi River

▲ Charles Mound
(1,235 feet/
376 m)

Rockford

Waukegan

Elgin

Cicero

Naperville

Chicago

Aurora

Joliet

Field Museum

Shedd Aquarium

Wrigley Field

John Deere
Pavilion
(Moline)

Starved Rock
State Park
(Utica)

N

Wildlife Prairie
State Park
(Hanna City)

Peoria

Morton

**Morton Pumpkin
Festival**

Champaign

Illinois River

Springfield

Illinois State Museum

**Abraham Lincoln
Presidential Library
and Museum**

INDIANA

Wabash River

MISSOURI

Cahokia Mounds State
Historic Site
(Collinsville)

Rend
Lake

Mississippi River

Ohio River

**Super
Museum**
(Metropolis)

Miles

0   20   40   60

0   40   80

Kilometers

KENTUCKY

ILLINOIS FACTS

NICKNAMES: Land of Lincoln, Prairie State

SONG: "Illinois" by C. H. Chamberlain and Archibald Johnston

MOTTO: "State Sovereignty, National Union"

> **FLOWER:** violet

TREE: white oak

> **BIRD:** cardinal

ANIMALS: white-tailed deer, painted turtle, eastern tiger salamander

> **FOODS:** goldrush apple, popcorn

DATE AND RANK OF STATEHOOD: December 3, 1818; the 21st state

> **CAPITAL:** Springfield

AREA: 57,918 square miles (150,007 sq. km)

AVERAGE JANUARY TEMPERATURE: 26°F (–3°C)

AVERAGE JULY TEMPERATURE: 76°F (24°C)

POPULATION AND RANK: 12,882,135; 5th (2013)

MAJOR CITIES AND POPULATIONS: Chicago (2,714,856), Aurora (199,932), Rockford (150,843), Joliet (148,268), Naperville (143,684)

NUMBER OF US CONGRESS MEMBERS: 19 representatives, 2 senators

NUMBER OF ELECTORAL VOTES: 21

NATURAL RESOURCES: limestone, clay, coal, fluorite, lead, zinc, oil, peat, tripoli

AGRICULTURAL PRODUCTS: soybeans, corn, hogs, cattle, wheat, oats, sorghum, hay, sheep, poultry, fruits, vegetables

MANUFACTURED GOODS: construction equipment, farm machinery, machine tools, baked goods, cereal, candy, sausage, soft drinks, cleaning solutions, pharmaceuticals

STATE HOLIDAYS AND CELEBRATIONS: Casimir Pulaski Day (first Monday in March), Lincoln's Birthday (February 12)

GLOSSARY

cast iron: a hard metal that is melted and poured into containers to make different shapes

catapult: a device for hurling objects

combine: a machine that cuts crops and separates the seeds from the plants

erode: to be worn away by water, wind, or glacial ice

exhibit: an article or a collection in a public showing

hatchery: a place where humans raise fish or chickens from eggs

immigrant: a person who moves to a different country

memorabilia: things valued or collected for their relation to a particular field or interest

mound: a small hill or heap of dirt or stones

plateau: a large, flat piece of land that sits higher than the land around it

simulator: a machine that is used to show what something feels or looks like

FURTHER INFORMATION

Birle, Pete. *Chicago Bulls*. La Jolla, CA: MVP Books, 2013. The Chicago Bulls have six championships under their belts, but they weren't always superstars. Learn more about Chicago's hometown NBA team and their rise to the top.

Cahokia Mounds State Historic Site
http://cahokiamounds.org
Get the scoop on this ancient city and how archaeologists discovered its existence.

Enjoy Illinois
http://www.enjoyillinois.com
Visit the official website of Illinois Tourism to plan your next visit to the Land of Lincoln. Explore activities by region, city, and month.

Ireland, Daniel. *Chicago: An Interactive Travel Guide for Kids.* Grand Haven, MI: Three Leaf Press, 2010. Go on a citywide scavenger hunt as you explore Chicago. Follow clues, complete tasks, and collect rewards while you explore everything the Windy City has to offer.

Schott, Jane A. *Abraham Lincoln*. Minneapolis: Lerner Publications, 2003. Learn more about Abraham Lincoln's life before he became president of the United States.

Starved Rock State Park
http://www.starvedrockstatepark.org
Learn about the history behind Starved Rock and its name.

INDEX

PHOTO ACKNOWLEDGMENTS

The images in this book are used with the permission of: © Songquan Deng/Shutterstock Images, p. 1; NASA, pp. 2–3; © Jessica Kirsh/Shutterstock Images, p. 4; © Wildnerdpix/Shutterstock Images, p. 5 (bottom); © Laura Westlund/Independent Picture Service, pp. 5 (top), 27; National Archives and Records Administration, p. 6; © Jason Patrick Ross/Shutterstock Images, pp. 6–7, 10–11; Chase Elliott Clark, p. 7; © Mike Liu/Shutterstock Images, pp. 8–9; © Max H Photo/Shutterstock Images, p. 9 (top); © Richard Cavalleri/Shutterstock Images, p. 9 (bottom); © Peter Wey/Shutterstock Images, p. 11 (top); © Owen Weber/Shutterstock Images, p. 11 (bottom); © Kim Karpeles/Alamy, pp. 12–13, 13 (top), 18–19; James Grant Wilson and John Fiske, p. 13 (bottom); © Dennis Donohue/Shutterstock Images, p. 14; © Constantin Stanciu/Shutterstock Images, pp. 14–15; © Igor Sh/Shutterstock Images, p. 15; © Shutterstock Images, pp. 16–17; © Mark Edward Atkinson/Thinkstock, p. 17 (top); © Justin O'Brien/The Gazette/AP Images, p. 17 (bottom); © Kravka/Shutterstock Images, p. 18; Highsmith (Carol M.) Archive/Library of Congress, p. 19 (LC-DIG-highsm-04515); National Park Service Digital Images Archives, pp. 20–21, 29 (bottom left); © R. Gino Santa Maria/Shutterstock Images, p. 21 (top); © Justin L. Fowler/The State Journal-Register/AP Images, p. 21 (bottom); © Vladislav Gajic/Shutterstock Images, p. 22; © Ira Block/National Geographic Society/Corbis, pp. 22–23; © Don Smetzer/Alamy, p. 23; David Wilson, pp. 24–25; © Andre Jenny/Alamy, p. 25 (top); © Andre Jenny Stock Connection Worldwide/Newscom, p. 25 (bottom); © nicoolay/iStockphoto, p. 26; © Jitchanamont/Shutterstock Images, p. 29 (top left); © Chris T Pehlivan/Shutterstock Images, p. 29 (top right); © AndersPhoto/Shutterstock Images, p. 29 (bottom right).

Cover: © iStockphoto.com/Kubrak 78 (Wrigley Field); © iStockphoto.com/chrisp0 (skyline); © iStockphoto.com/vandervelden (tractor); © Laura Westlund/Independent Picture Service (map); © iStockphoto.com/fpm (seal); © iStockphoto.com/vicm (pushpins); © iStockphoto.com/benz190 (corkboard).